FRANCES ZWEIFEL

Animal Baby-Sitters

illustrated by Irene Brady

William Morrow and Company
New York 1981

Printed in the United States of America.
1 2 3 4 5 6 7 8 9 10

Library of Congress Cataloging in Publication Data

Zweifel, Frances W
    Animal baby-sitters.
    Summary: Explains how cows, elephants, macaques, and acorn woodpeckers
function as babysitters, thus helping animal parents raise their young.
    1. Parental behavior in animals—Juvenile literature. [1. Parental behavior
in animals. 2. Animals—Habits and behavior] I. Brady, Irene. II. Title.
QL762.Z86   591.56   80-39719
ISBN 0-688-00443-1   ISBN 0-688-00444-X (lib. bdg.)

To Joan Weatherby of Animas, New Mexico,
who introduced me to animal baby-sitters.

On a ranch in New Mexico, the cattle are coming in for water. They walk slowly toward the corral, one behind the other. Many of the cows have little calves by their sides.

The first cow in line, an old red one, has no calf. She stops by the corral gate. One by one, the mother cows pass her. They walk to the water tank inside the corral, but their calves stay behind with Old Red, outside the gate.

One little calf kicks up his heels. He playfully butts his head at another calf. Old Red looks at the mischief-maker and shakes her head up and down, up and down. The calf backs away and stands still. Now all the calves wait quietly with Old Red while their mothers get a long, cool drink.

As each cow leaves the corral, she collects her own calf. (The calves do not need water; they get enough in their mothers' milk.) Cow and calf move off a little way to wait for the others. Finally, Old Red is free to get a drink of water for herself.

What is going on here? Is Old Red really baby-sitting?

Yes, indeed! The old red cow is a baby-sitter. She watches over the calves every time the herd comes to the corral for water.

These cows are range cattle. Unlike dairy cows, they live in herds that roam freely and sometimes for long distances. Range cows must rely on each other for help in raising their calves.

R. B. Townshend was an Englishman who became an American cowboy. He worked in Texas in the second half of the nineteenth century. Later he wrote about his adventures among the Texas longhorn cattle.

One day Townshend saw a herd of longhorns
drinking at a river. Cattle usually like to stay near cool
water during the hot part of the day. This time, however, six cows walked quickly away from the river.
Townshend was curious about them and decided to
follow them.

He rode with the cows for several miles. They went up into the sandy hills above the river. There Townshend found a "regular nursery," where two old longhorn cows were guarding eight little calves. When the six cows appeared, they called to their calves. Six of the calves ran to their mothers and soon were nursing hungrily. Now the two baby-sitters could go for water. Off they went, leaving their own two little calves behind for the other cows to guard.

Townshend was surprised to learn that cows can be baby-sitters. But cows are not the only animals that baby-sit. All over the world many kinds of animals are helping animal parents raise their children.

Social animals like cows live together in groups of their own kind. Some of the names of these animal groups are "herds," "troops," "bands," and "flocks." The animals in the group have friends and relations nearby. These friends and relations sometimes can be good baby-sitters.

Not all social animals can use baby-sitters. Horses, for instance, live in herds, but they do not have baby-sitters. The mother horse cannot leave her foal. The baby horse nurses from its mother two or three times each hour. But the cow's calf can wait several hours between feedings as it drinks more milk at one time. So the calf can stay with a baby-sitter while its mother goes away.

Scientists call animal baby-sitters "aunts." This name does not mean the baby-sitter is actually the sister of one of the parents. It only means that she cares for the baby animal in the same way your human auntie would care for you.

Another animal that lives in a herd is the African elephant. An elephant herd is a matriarchy [*may*-tree-ar-kee]; the members of the herd are adult females and their young ones. Grandmother elephant is the leader of the herd.

Like human children, the little elephant has a "teen-age" baby-sitter. This young female elephant may choose a special baby to watch over from the moment it is born.

A mother elephant is about to give birth. Several other members of her herd stand around her. One of these onlookers is a teen-age female.

The 200-pound baby is born. It lies on the ground, all wrinkled and crumpled-looking. Its tired mother stands nearby, swaying slightly. The other elephants press closer. Then the young female moves to the baby and stands over it. She protects it from being kicked or trampled by the huge, 5000-pound adults.

While the baby elephant is very young, it stays close to its mother. The baby-sitter lingers nearby. Sometimes she comes too close; the mother elephant pushes her aside so the baby can nurse.

A few months later the baby elephant is stronger and more agile. Now it can leave its mother's side to play with the other calves in the herd. The young female follows along. When the playing becomes too rough, a fight starts. The baby-sitter slips into the group of little roughnecks and nudges her special calf away to safety.

One day, when the herd stops to rest, the little elephant falls asleep in the shade of a tree. When the other elephants are ready to move on, the baby is still sleeping. Slowly the herd begins to wander down the trail. The baby's auntie is worried. What if her little charge gets left behind? She goes quickly to the napping baby and touches it. She has to shake it to wake it up. Together they run down the trail to join their herd.

Male and female elephant calves play together when they are young. They bump and slap and ram into one another. But as they grow older, the females lose interest in such rough play. Instead, they like to take care of younger calves.

Young male elephants continue to fight with each other. By the age of ten or twelve, they are so rowdy that they are driven out of their herd. Now they must wander alone or join a smaller herd of other bachelors.

Elephants live fifty years or more. A large part of their life is spent in their mother's herd. There they learn their most important lessons: where the best food grows, where to find water, where the safe trails are. And their baby-sitter is one of their best teachers.

Many kinds of monkeys, like these baboons, have baby-sitters too. Often the aunt is the baby's older sister. Or the baby-sitter may be the mother monkey's best friend.

In the forests of Japan, however, there are monkeys known as macaques [ma-*kaks*] who use a different kind of baby-sitter. Dr. Junichiro Itani is a scientist who has studied these Japanese monkeys. Dr. Itani found that some macaque troops have *uncles* instead of aunts.

Summer is the time when Japanese macaques are born. The mother monkeys cuddle their new babies, nurse them, and carry them around. In a few weeks, the little ones are old enough to play with one another. But their mothers still keep them very close.

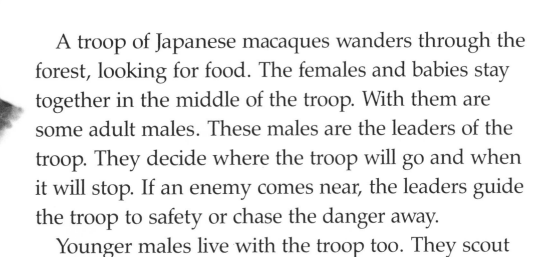

A troop of Japanese macaques wanders through the forest, looking for food. The females and babies stay together in the middle of the troop. With them are some adult males. These males are the leaders of the troop. They decide where the troop will go and when it will stop. If an enemy comes near, the leaders guide the troop to safety or chase the danger away.

Younger males live with the troop too. They scout ahead when the troop moves and watch out for enemies. These young males usually do not stay near the females and babies.

Autumn comes and then winter. Food is scarce. The weather turns cold, and snow falls. The young monkeys huddle close to their mothers to keep warm.

At last spring comes. The time of hunger and cold is over. While their mothers watch closely, the young monkeys play together.

Before long, one mother macaque gives birth to a baby. More Japanese monkeys are born. Soon almost all the adult females are busy with new babies, too busy to take care of their one-year-old young. There are not enough females left to become aunts. Sad and lonely, the one-year-old monkeys begin to wander.

Now the male leaders of the Japanese monkey troop come to their rescue. In a little while, all the young monkeys have uncles. The uncles hold the young macaques, walk with them, and groom their fur. They help the youngsters find food and protect them from danger. Males usually are rough and bad tempered, but these uncles act like gentle aunts.

When the birth season is over, the young macaques go back to their mothers. But now the youngsters recognize the adult males as friends in their troop. The caring of the uncles has helped to bind this troop together and make it stronger.

Animal baby-sitters can be found in the air, too. Birds who help mothers and fathers raise their young are called "helpers at the nest." These helpers may be the real aunts and uncles of the baby birds, or they may be their older brothers and sisters.

Flocks of acorn woodpeckers live in the western United States, Mexico, and Central America. Scientists have studied these little birds and found that a whole flock of woodpeckers takes care of one nest of babies.

The acorn woodpecker flock has only one pair of
parent birds. But all the adult members of the flock
help to make the nest. Together they clean out a hole
in a tree. The mother bird lays her eggs in the hole.
Then all the adults incubate the eggs. They take turns,
making sure that there is always a parent or helper to
sit on the eggs and keep them warm.

In about two weeks, the eggs hatch. The parents and helpers bring food to the nestlings. They take turns staying in the nest with the babies; everyone gets a chance to baby-sit.

When the baby woodpeckers are five weeks old, they can fly. Soon these fledglings learn to catch insects for themselves.

At the end of summer, there are green acorns for the woodpeckers to eat. The young birds do not know how to open an acorn. They must learn from their parents and the helpers.

The young birds learn how to store acorns, too. The adult woodpecker drills a hole in a tree, then jams an acorn into the hole, pointed end in. The young woodpecker copies its teacher. In this way, the woodpecker flock stores up enough acorns to last the whole winter.

In the spring, there is another nest of baby acorn woodpeckers. Last year's young are all grown up. Now they will be helpers at the nest for the flock's new babies.

All around the world there are many kinds of animal baby-sitters. These animal aunts are important to their herd or troop or flock. They may bring extra food to the baby animals. They teach the young how to find food. They protect the little ones from harm while their mothers are away. And the baby-sitters help the youngsters make friends and strengthen their group.

Animal baby-sitters do even more than help the baby animals. Young baby-sitters are practicing to become good animal parents. Soon the time will come when they will need baby-sitters of their own.

BIBLIOGRAPHY

Douglas-Hamilton, Iain and Oria.
Among the Elephants.
New York: Viking Press, 1975.
Itani, Junichiro.
"Paternal Care in the Wild Japanese Monkey, *Macaca fuscata*."
Primate Social Behavior, An Enduring Problem,
edited by Charles H. Southwick.
New York: Van Nostrand Reinhold Co., 1963.
MacRoberts, Michael H. and Barbara R.
"Social Organization and Behavior of the Acorn Woodpecker
in Central Coastal California."
Ornithological Monographs, No. 21.
The American Ornithologists' Union, 1976.
Townshend, R.B.
A Tenderfoot in Colorado.
London: The Bodley Head, Ltd., 1923.
Wilson, Edward O.
Sociobiology.
Cambridge: Harvard University Press, 1975.